THE SIREN
WORLD

JUAN J. MORALES

THE SIREN WORLD
Copyright © 2015 Juan J. Morales

ISBN 978-0-9962170-0-2

Design and layout: Harvey-Rosen.

LITHIC PRESS
fine books for an old planet

www.lithicpress.com

ACKNOWLEDGEMENTS

Many thanks to the editors of the following publications, where these poems appeared or are forthcoming, sometimes in slightly different or in revised forms:

Acentos Review—Excerpts from "Epistles to El Inca Garcilaso de la Vega"

Anti- —Excerpt from "Guaman Poma, Writing by Candlelight"

Border Senses—Excerpt from "Guaman Poma, Writing by Candlelight"

Casa de Cinco Hermanas—"Scars"

Catch-Up—"El Condor Pasa"

Copper Nickel—"Smallpox"

The Cossack—"Talking to the Dead"

Crab Orchard Review—"Gift"

Duende— "A Place That No Longer Exists" & "Downtown Ambato, 3:14 AM,"

Fickle Muses— "Searching for the Lost Fountain of Cuzco"

Fruita Pulp—"The Siren World" & "Found Poem…"

Gris-Gris—"Subterfuge," "The Death of Don Francisco Pizarro," & "The Descendents Who Slipped through History's Fingers, 1539"

Hinchas de Poesia—"The Cursing Chorus of the Mob"

Huizache—"Discovering Pain" & "First Time in Ecuador"

Iron Horse Literary Review—"A Good Education"

The New Gnus—"Rendering the Voice of Atahualpa" & "Spare Change"

North Dakota Review—"New World Map"

Poet Lore—"Passport"

Route 7 Review—"The Documentaries I've Seen" & "Illapa and Questions of Belief"

Sugar House Review—"The Disease and Two Labs"

Washington Square—"Empire"

Write On! SCWP's 2007 SI Anthology—"Garter Snakes"

Personal thanks to all my friends at Colorado State University-Pueblo, my students, the Wallyball Bunch, BTP, Dawg Patch United, my Pilgrimage comrades, Jonathan Bohr Heinen, Gary Jackson, Lisa Hase Jackson, Melody Gee, Scott Gage, Cynthia & Ted Taylor, Alysse Kathleen McCanna, Sandra Beasley, Jim Daniels, Rigoberto González, David Keplinger, Lisa D. Chavez, and my fellow artists, kickballers, gamers, musicians, and friends in P-town.

Shout out to my CantoMundo familia, Francisco Aragón, Pintura : Palabra, Samuel Miranda, and Con Tinta, who inspired me when I discovered many of these poems.

To my fellow Goatheads: Iver Arnegard, Juliana Aragón Fatula, and Maria Kelson for their invaluable feedback on these poems and book.

To Danny Rosen and Kyle Harvey at Lithic Press for making this book.

Finally, love to my family: Mom, Dad, Esther, Sydney, Regan, Glenn, Rosita, Rafael, Gwyneth, Thais, Carmen, Alex, todos en Ecuador y Puerto Rico, the Freemans, Alyssa, Carrie, and especially my partner in crime, Patti, who I couldn't do this without.

I. THE MOUNTAIN

II. THE ISLAND

THE SIREN WORLD

"Our duty…is to express what is unheard of. Everything has been painted in Europe, everything has been sung in Europe. But not in America."

—Pablo Neruda, "The Lamb and the Pinecone"

I. THE MOUNTAIN

A GOOD EDUCATION

As a girl in Ecuador, my mother recited saints, prayers, and science formulas.

Our reports in Social Studies did the same when we studied places like Ecuador and commonwealths like Puerto Rico,

served up imports, exports, populations, flags in class with poster board markered and spilled glue.

The world's violence fell from minds like pencils dropped under ancient radiators.

It's all about patriotism learned in a classroom, my mother admiring the Incan King Atahualpa and shaking her head at brother Huáscar.

Lessons widened the divide with Peru, the other country.

Amazing how civil war boils between brothers, flaring up battlegrounds no one can pinpoint.

The blame game helped my mom and her class imagine the disputed zone, el oriente, that divides two countries, that bends young, confused thoughts that clamped inside her, tight fists balled in pride.

And I put myself there too,

getting a good education, oblivious to our country's failings, saying the pledge of allegiance and gawking up at the flag with my small hand on my heart, about which

I knew nothing.

GIFT

*

Take the middle-aged man in an Albuquerque laundromat
who once asked me about my ancestry and boasted

of his 15th generation Spanish heritage held on tracts of land he had
claim to in New Mexico or Spain. I don't remember which.

When I tell him my parents never taught me Spanish, he instructs me
with the condescending click of a tongue to learn.

His tone enough to redden my face like a slap he would have obliged
when I already implicate myself enough in the form

of awkward conjugations and the repeated phrase "¿Cómo se dice...?"
Thinking about it now, this man showed me

how we can associate ourselves with one side
and deny the conquered half. I wish I could ask him now

if he knows how we can forgive
the culmination in our struggle through words and idiomas.

*

Bestowed with identical names, the forgotten family are doppelgangers
wearing similar expressions in weathered photos, high cheekbones,
stares of the denied indigena.

I look into their eyes by staring in the mirror and witness
the wounds of younger days I regret collecting.

When I was fourteen and asked if we had Indian blood inside,
my mother's point blank answer, "No." Even then, I didn't believe,

angry she didn't understand why it mattered to recognize
two bloods swirled together while I didn't consider how

concealing the indigena protected her growing up in Ecuador.
To forget the native within, to smother origins in denial,
are adopted habits

from times before I knew how to track a pen into words.
I think about my confusion burying me on a line

drawn in the sand, knowing it will be erased
by the rising tide, and then I turn again

to write future and past pressed together as the skin
we wish to crawl out of, but have to accept as a gift.

A PLACE THAT NO LONGER EXISTS

My alpaca tapestry composes
an empire, then and now. The hands
that made and sold it to me,
a younger man, for fifteen dollars
on a quiet roadside
between Quito and Otavalo.

Or was it Ambato and Quito?
I admire precise shapes
of llamas and lizards and men. I find
the wear of approaching rips,
discoloration, loosened strands
I will not tug.

The red and black and white
stained wool shuttle expansion
and tributaries, but the tapestry conceals
the shape of the land before any tourists,
before the Old World arrived,
before cracks bloomed on the asphalt.

The sun always touches the small town's houses
now derelict or replaced. The tapestry:
evidence of the road and town
I will find again even if
the tapestry falls to ruin in
what no longer exists.

THE SIREN WORLD

I hear translated calls.
Terms for birds snatch
moths, rivers smother
mountains, skies fused into
mouths like alloys.

My mind's resistance
to pluck new words from the air
is naïve, but I fight how my tongue
twists in awkward positions
until it naturalizes to speech.

The world seduces me to be
the conquistador who strips armor on the beach,
consents to clothes
tattering off his frame,
ghosts into foliage,

and when opening my mouth to speak,
English, Spanish,
Quichua, Quechua
send me careening into
the smashed rocks of language.

TALKING TO THE DEAD

Be careful. They grow weak when you ask them too much. Their croons in ductwork and walls will wane. Don't drown them out in electronic frequencies or ignore their language of clicking pipes and creaking doors. Be alert. Listen. This is not automatic writing or a way to neglect your own voice. You're at your desk, replacing the empty memory spools with new threads. Let speeches of the dead weave strings into tapestries. Warm yourself under the coarse knits of a blanket assembled by weary hands and eyes, with the dead coaxing you to continue laboring with them in the weakly lit room, in a place beyond sleep.

GUAMAN POMA, WRITING BY CANDLELIGHT

*Guaman Poma (1560-1616) A Quechua noble known for his chronicle
in which he denounced the ill treatment of the natives of the Andes after
the Spanish Conquest.*

He thumbs the folio of
sun children one last time.
When writing, he instructs himself
to flatter the King, to hide displeasure
between lines, to rouse
with flags into the colony's ownership,
laws of God and man
to declare Indians as Peru's true masters.

Soon after, Guaman Poma will
meet the courier who will carry shaky trust
in swollen purse. His released book
will become a voice
passed through hands that will stow it
in the misplaced slivers of history.

And he thinks of the folio
crumbling in a fist of flames,
or the ink eventually drowning
in stacks of browning pages, but not before
the King of Spain leafs through,
panging anger in his heart.
He tries to erase thoughts of
the expected messenger, clutching
knife and royal sealed envelope in hand.

What he does not envision
is four hundred quiet years
before the book emerges

unread in the Copenhagen library stacks
between yellowed tomes.

Where will my words about Guaman Poma be lost?
Maybe an attic, a thick folder in a desk,
or a garage box, but still confident
in the risky release of poems
into the hands of a comrade
who will carry each sacred word,
chancing the indifferent someone
who will never bother to read.

THE PRISONERS OF LITORAL

Ecuador, June 20, 2005

I am a prisoner of Litoral—
    detained with a thousand crowded others
    cells absent of light and water.

I've lingered in my cell all along—
    police never charged me, my lawyer never showed,
    never stepped into any courtroom.

I'm buried up to my neck in the yard—
    "The living dead"—I chant with the hopeless chorus.
    Sun pounds down. Dirt blows into my mouth.

I punish myself—
    tapped nails into my wrists and ankles, straight through.
    Guards cringe. Press afraid to intervene.

I sew my lips shut with black thread—
    punishing my flesh for clothes and food,
    stealing back from the droves of rats.

We sing for the prisoners of Litoral—
    penned-up beasts writing on placards in blood,
    afraid of our protests fading, backs pressed against walls.

DISCOVERING PAIN

I was sixteen and skateboarding on a failed double-kick flip, ankle's loud pop. I went on with my day in the swell of pain, small ankle bone floating with snapped cartilage, one of the first moments of learning my fragility. I used to always sacrifice body and told myself, "It'll heal, no worries." Now, I sometimes bang a finger or suffer a magnificent garden scratch and claim them for the attention. But in instances with more at stake, moments of failing family or mourning love's purest hurt, I am paralyzed to speak. Perhaps this paradox, hiding in the open, helps me study my obsessions, like conquests centuries earlier, the Incan reign coming undone as an ache I did not witness but read in the Andes and in pages. I am guided toward historical pain, a shrine built on the journey to museums, the pondering of a PBS documentary on Friday night, a National Geographic in a waiting room eerily similar to Bishop's childhood memory, the untouched structures still buried around Machu Picchu, but what happens when the hurt I reference involves a skateboard, an ankle, or a childhood's bloodied kneecap, minor images hundreds of years later and still a continent removed, coming too late, coming too late?

SMALLPOX

Ten days straight, the slave
has longed to steady the sea, hammock,
fever's spike. Another holds

his head, sponges his body.
Blisters swell from his mouth,
torso, legs, like settling dust.

When his eyesight fails, the slave
complains of the fuming sweet,
water throb against pores.

Every day chains
the disease between the slaves.
He becomes a vessel

from across the sea, carried
past ports to the mainland
where he will taint

runners and kings into
bodies sapped and writhing
on woven mats.

When it no longer needs him,
the disease leeches over everything
without thought, poisons

the mother's caress, suffocates
the air of town meetings. The sprawl
an unseen army with no compass.

A KIND OF CHEMISTRY

Buried in tundra,
near the small village vanished
before civilization, a body of an Inuit girl
collapses with the stains of smallpox.
Her hands out like a fallen swimmer
or someone fleeing her own shadow.
Frozen until discovered and parsed up
by an archaic science,

she is a forgotten arm jarred in alcohol.
The store room's heater gnarls flesh and bone into
mummy stasis until two virologists
discover her and
cajole the genetics of smallpox
out of hiding.

They extract a kind of chemistry that unifies it all
into understanding
of how a girl's arm pieces
time in concert. A cure.
Without her, the science would be as distant as her scars,
but at what point did an inoculated population,
like all of us, rubbing a fresh injection,
dismiss her as a fascinating specimen
we never knew?

INOCULATION

The old Ft. Carson hospital,
WWII era building, wood worn and peeling white—
my parents proffered me for annual physicals.
I carried my green chart with bold lettering, a kid who
trusted military protocol to lead me
and other army brats through florescent hallways,
past the impatient coughs of pharmacy patients,
with nurses in the chaos of scrubs, and to doctors
with BDU's and stethoscope necks.
Somewhere between forms and Q & A and
rolled-up sleeves, the injection entering.

I looked away to wince, fear of it hitting
bone or puncturing all the way through.
The vaccine did nothing
I could feel within,
and the doctor took out
my yellow card from the file
to write date, time, year, name.
Inoculated, but not against
the poke and grab of clinical hands.

THE DISEASE AND TWO LABS

Imagine two labs, the CDC and the one in Siberia
both behind checkpoints.
Like in the movies: flasks, files, microscopes set each scene.
Technicians in Hazmats manipulate
microbes behind thick glass.
Extinction circles for the disease that altered

histories and trajectories.
Suits and lab coats debate its preservation/destruction,
and, in impassioned speeches, they ask you
to imagine smallpox never infecting another man, woman, or child
versus counterpoints who
take stock of the unaccounted

specimens, rogue labs, inoculation samples
in old hospitals, or unfound bodies in limbo. You're no scientist
and you might have formed an opinion,
but you can't shake doomsday scenarios
that accompany each decision they will make
without consulting you.

THE DOCUMENTARIES I'VE SEEN

"Historians are gossips who lease the dead."
—Voltaire

They are no match for stories fueled
by coffee and book excavations. I nod off to scholars
standing beside walls or sitting
in plush studies as they accompany
narrations over the graphics of
how armies navigated terrain. The color-coded
arrows of a tribe's migratory patterns
through on-screen maps
where inches equal miles. I translate
diagrams into the march.
Educational reenactments use
accurate costumes, settings, but even
the good actors just aren't right.
I sigh at edited time slots between
tire commercials and promos.
I'm hoping for useful statistics and keep
a peripheral eye out for ambushes,
the wounded killed on salted earth.
Late at night, in dreams constructed by
the guttural howls of men within New World trees,
I wake to the dark screen,
the credits rolled, and
new questions forcing me to admit
after hours of watching and re-watching,
I can't understand why we insist on sequencing—
conquest to invasion to occupation.

RENDERING THE VOICE OF ATAHUALPA

"But they pulled me out of a sack,
and they stuck me together with glue."
                                   —*Sylvia Plath*

I died opened by a blade and in the fire hot of foreign men's
        breath only to wake up as pieces of the people, you who
        brought me back in murals and embedded texts.

I am a bullheaded bastard with no right to rule, out of touch
        with my subjects.

I am your mural of a decapitated head in the hands of a
        dignified man, an upright body sitting at a feast. My
        neck sprays like a majestic fountain.

I am the last king before the Inca fell, a prodigy on a chesboard,
        who taught invaders our people were not ignorant
        heathens to dismiss.

In an obscure rendering, I am the façade painted with a proud
        sneer next to a man I don't know, Bolívar, and Ché in a
        Quito schoolyard above the black top basketball courts.
        You are the children who glance up and go back to
        playing.

SUBTERFUGE

In the wreckage of job well done,
Pizarro and his generals sorted
gold and silver into shares
like children devouring unknown delicacies
described only by eccentric adults.
They recalled how hopeless steps
guided them through vacant stomachs
and cracked lips to victory.
Their gambles paying off.
They gorged on exaggerated chunks
stuck between gnashing, stumbled
fits of laughter.

They pre-enacted a president
posturing behind a podium on an aircraft carrier,
dark suit and blood red tie.
He's posed with thumbs-up in front of
the "Mission Accomplished" banner
on a stars and stripes backdrop
with flag-draped coffins piling
out of view and stacks of condolence letters
for his aides to stamp.
We jeered the President,

but in the case of conquistadors,
no one snapped the ironic picture
of men snaking spoils
into hidden pockets whenever comrades
blinked. They embraced, ready
to dream of being old, rich men because
that's what they were supposed to do.

THE CURSING CHORUS OF THE MOB

During a visit home to the states, my brother described a family of brujas in Ecuador, a province south of Quito, in our mother's hometown, who hexed their neighborhood for ransoms with ingested powders and the hanging of haunted charms. They bled everyone dry until the neighbors, tired of superstition, became the ski-masked mob who kicked down doors, ransacked rooms, and massacred the grandmothers, mothers, daughters, and nieces in shotgun blasts and splattered walls. Everyone knew the guilty parties who mingled when the police arrived to find the bodies and zipped mouths of witnesses. I didn't say anything to my brother, but I couldn't help thinking, even if we won't admit it, maybe our fears of wickedness can provoke us to embrace the rage that grows tall enough to unhinge ceilings and touch the tips of the eucalyptus trees surrounding Ambato. Maybe we could be driven to inflict violence against those who prick the back of our necks or cause our phantom aches and to sing with the cursing chorus that emerges as a devouring wave to make someone, or anyone, pay with the blood we carry every fucking day.

THE DEATH OF FRANCISCO PIZARRO

June 26, 1541—
"Here is the skull of the Marquis Don Francisco Pizarro who
discovered and won Peru and placed it under the crown of Castile."

In the after dinner ambush,
you met death
via rapiers and daggers:
defense wounds,
neck thrusts, nicked
vertebra, damaged sphenoid,
and an eye socket
punctured through
by the points of
betrayed men, reaping
a bit of what you had sown.
You got lucky
with your horse-driven sorcery
until you were left
to cross yourself
then to kiss
your blood-caked
right hand, last breath.
We forget
your headless body
buried in the cathedral's
special chapel,
head housed in
the inscribed lead box.

FOUND POEM TAPED TO A CLOSED PIZZA PARLOR WINDOW, AUSTIN, TX

New World—
Your key will open the gold
padlock. Please re-chain
and lock when
you leave. Call out
for further instructions.

SEARCHING FOR THE LOST FOUNTAIN IN CUZCO

If I lived hundreds of years ago
I would have begged passersby to exhume
the temple's lost fountainhead,
where sacred water
once rose from unknown wells.
I would have asked them to spare water
for our desiccated gardens
even in the absence of flowers.

Cursed those
who subtracted pious flagstones
and wished throats
filled with silt
to mourn forgotten waters
below Cuzco's foundation.

I would have apologized
to those who never quenched
thirst. Scolded parents
for failing to recall the network
of gold pipes under
Cuzco's haciendas and jagged streets
and asked, how will our children ever taste
a fresh lick of rain offered
by the Gods?

THE DESCENDENTS WHO SLIPPED THROUGH HISTORY'S FINGERS, 1539

In towns around the navel of the earth
they emerge

features of two continents
born to laze together.

Boys and girls molded in anatomies
with Old and New World bloods

unified through arteries and tiny hearts.
The high cheekbones and tan complexions

flare against fathers' fair hair
and blue eyes.

They are children who stop loving tunics
swaddled around,

curious of the fathers
departing in pursuit of heavier purses.

No one knows to call them new children
of genetics. They arrive

in papers and castes:
miraculous histories hidden

in colonial crowds,
multiplying over the hemisphere.

EL CONDOR PASA

Not the Simon and Garfunkel one.
For my mom, it was the original
on an old record click started to position,
the needle that summoned wood flutes
to breathe slow notes followed
by the plucked guitars, harbored
the image of the dark-shaped bird in pale sky.

Growing up, I never understood
how in her mind and in song, the condor glides
currents of sound, hanging above snowy peaks,
open wings glistening like
the record's black grooves. I never followed
why she played the song daily
and hummed the melody when she didn't,

swaying her to a dance through the house.
Even hearing "El Condor Pasa"
in a museum parking lot in Albuquerque,
played by two hitchhiking Ecuadorians or
in an Otavalo discoteque
when I was eighteen, I couldn't
hum along. It wasn't until much later,

once I didn't hear the song anymore,
that I appreciated it as anthem
encased in the somber hiss
of the plastic '45, that black circle halting,
the bird as a distant V
still adrift on wind,
forever in my mind.

EPISTLES TO EL INCA GARCILASO DE LA VEGA

Garcilaso de la Vega (1539–1616), also known as El Inca, was a chronicler and writer from the Spanish Viceroyalty of Peru. The son of a Spanish conquistador and Inca noblewoman, he is recognized primarily for his contributions to Inca history, culture, and society.

*

In that moment when you first
spotted Spain,
after months of the sun's glib dips,
you thought about your father
in Peru's sacred ground
and wanted to spit.

He sent you through the
unstable cycle of tutors who shaped you
into an Old World gentleman,
an imposter, troubled by
your homeland memories
and swallowed
in a terrifying city
with alien steeples and slanting streets.

*

You turned away callers
when the old language drummed
between bones.
Your dreams howled
like a childhood memory
sending you to hide
in home's distant chambers.

You failed to flatter
Spanish dukes with your father's
capricious loyalty
pinned to your name.
Every time you assumed
Peru's voice,
conjoined in laurels and smoke,

you locked yourself
in the trauma of a fire-filled home
to rip ink along pages
with the forbearers sweating you
to avoid a future of
dust collected on your
broken clocks.

*

You did not have many
possessions scattered through your sparse
apartment—frayed quills
near inkwells encrusted
black, hoarded
heaps of manuscripts.

You called yourself El Inca,
self-appointed, self-ostracized.
Peru was the abandoned
place in your scribbles,
into your flesh that catenated two worlds,
overlooked like your left-behind property
that no one wanted.

And writing in my own time,
I, too, am haunted by the dirges
you wrote and how
they could never
take you home.

EMPIRE

Every first encounter
started as unrehearsed communiqué,
defined by charming smiles
that gleamed
until bartered wants
bubbled into tension beyond greed.
Eventually, misunderstandings
encroached into
nothing that could be wished away:
apologies
for a man's severed hands.

It was a desert of wars
that spread to the hemisphere's
alcoves like small plants sucking
drops from moisture-lipped land.
And when frontiers closed, it was not quick.
It grew into a new body branched
with new borders, digging in itself
to marrow out answers,
to conquer the forests of cells and blood,
to inject a new identity
in an ancient place.

SPARE CHANGE

Leaving a bowling alley, a man asked for some spare change. He looked dehydrated from milling in the sweltering July heat and wore a sleeveless denim shirt. I noticed his shoulder with the green feather tattoo, an eagle feather slanted down. After I shook out my pockets and told him I didn't have change, he asked my name. "Morales." He told me, "Leyba." I nodded and in that awkward introduction thought about shaking his hand, but I didn't. I walked away. Behind me, he mumbled, "mother fucker," and called after me, "Hey, we're all Indian, man."

ILLAPA AND QUESTIONS OF BELIEF

The word illapa means lightning, thunder,
and bolts to designate struck places,
sanctums to never be worshipped and sealed for good.
When the Spaniards opened one with prying tools,
los indigenas waited outside for
the fight of mutable clouds and lightening
that bathed the rooms in flames to kill
the nonbelievers. It's my reminder of abandoned Gods
lurking nearby, in the unreliable debris of time,
bumping shoulders with our modern world
and watching over the ones too stubborn
to stop believing. The story carries resistance
like a secret language that says the war
may have been fought, but the people will not
release their ties, gripping
deathbed relics into the afterlife.
How can I not believe what they believe?

RECONSTRUCTION SONG

Whether writing on a typewriter or living in 1599,
every letter is rationed.
To rip a page deadly.

It takes a thousand voices to tell a single story
with mumbling, back talk, manifestos brought to life
like your breath freed through a conch.

Host them in satchels that outlast humidity and
boxes etched with ornate drawings
of globes and flowers. Away from the elemental grind.

Treat it as a prayer
for bribed couriers who don't care
how the earth lurches. When you don't feel it either,

stop for a second. Place your hands
on the ground to accept time.
When you're ready, pry open

what is not forgotten and assemble
your polished words
sharper than knife points.

Tunnel them into our hearts
just before apathy makes our children
deaf to the army of voices you're meant to transcribe.

FIRST TIME IN ECUADOR

Quito, 1994

Because I could not speak any Spanish,
my trouble was deciphering things they
shared: fruit-like tomatoes in a cracked dish,

a glass of warm milk with a salty taste.
For dinner, they sat us at the table,
gave us forks, spoons, bowls, a normal routine.

Voices roared, the words impenetrable.
Stirring my soup, I found pig ears with beans.
I quieted, fearing each bite—thick fat

and coarse black hairs that scrape along my tongue.
I chewed small bites to taste this place, poked at
their offering. Being alone and young

made me reach for home, but I never ceased
wanting each meal to become our shared feast.

DOWNTOWN AMBATO, 3:14 AM

My mother's hometown,
surrounded by achingly beautiful mountains,
chills me. I am awake thinking about
stories of her childhood swallowed up
by an earthquake and the town
drowning in a celebration
of flowers every year afterward.
I am an apathetic teenager listening to
a strange store alarm
that blares every hour until
the sleepy vendor opens
the metal gate and shuts it off.

The Chinese restaurant's sign
across the street
shines blue and red, so I count
the time between the exhalations
of my mother asleep on the other side of the room.
I wait for stray dogs to bark
on cue, wishing they'd curl up
on a stoop somewhere on the block
and shut up. I turn in the bed every few minutes
and mangle my limbs in sheets
that scratch lullaby
out of my head.

Store alarm again
reverberates off unfinished rooftops
made of cement and rebar,
decorated with potted flowers and
clotheslines full of laundry.
For a moment, with my eyes closed,
I capture every town sound
and convince myself that I understand

my mother's hunger for sleep after so many years
without. Then I multiply it. I wish I could wake her
and ask how to say insomnia
in Spanish except hope
she's in the midst of peaceful sleep.

II. THE ISLAND

PEELING AN ORANGE

My short nails rip globe's flesh. In my kitchen
unfurling the peel into pieces long
undone, I spread them along the table like a map.
Each break of skin creates continents—
borders and topography taking shape.
Fleck islands strewn into fictitious seas, hide
resources to discover.

Thinking back—
King Carlos V perusing maps and dreaming
of flat-papered domains he'd never touch.
He helps me understand the invention of place
by hands and chance and how I participate in
the cartography of an unknown country before
knowing how deep it really delves, before
breaking into its nourishing pieces
slipped in mouth, flesh torn
and swallowed. Rinds and peels live
for a moment on my table,
and I choose one of them as the home of my family,
then sweep them aside.

PASSPORT

After Adál's "El Puerto Rican Passport, El Spirit Republic de Puerto Rico"

Cover Two rolled dice, both landing on three's. It looks like one from the U.S., calling out Republic of Puerto Rico.

Apellido (Morales) Two fruits my father's birthplace has bequeathed me are not sweet: expensive plane tickets and long flights back stateside. But the salted plátanos and aguacate mingle in my mouth. I wonder if my father still feels la isla home. I will not ask.

Nombre (Juan Jose) Combined with Morales, I travel with a name ripe for detainments. More than once, I re-enter through a waiting room full of scared and pissed off travelers. Customs agents let me go after I lift my sleeve to reveal the tattoo I don't have. Welcoming me back and telling me that my parents should have been more original with my name. My mom later apologizes.

Nacionalidad (Puerto-Rican/Ecuadorian/American) My father calls me gringito when we're on the island, and cousins do the same when they ask me to eat whatever's mixed in with the rice. I accept myself as a tourist, laboring to tack Spanish words together, my accent the scratchy throat I cannot clear.

Sexo (Male) When I turned 18, my father gave me a machete. When I turned 21, my father gave me a shoe shine kit.

Fecha de Nacimiento (11/15/1980) I was ten, in the Bronx, outside of a church for a cousin's wedding, the last time I saw my grandfather. He handed me a fresh $100 dollar bill. "For all your birthdays," my father translated.

Lugar de Nacimiento (Iowa City, Iowa) My father once called Puerto Rico the heartland, *tierra de mi corazon,* and joked with me to never take his ashes there when he died. "I was born there," he said, "and maybe we'll go back when I'm a hundred."

Fecha de Expedicion (First time in Puerto Rico) The Pomeranian my grandfather kept on a rope was a mean son of a bitch that snapped at everyone. I hugged the dog and tugged at its tail. It protected me, but my grandfather insisted he would bury it where it laid if it growled even once.

Fecha de Caducidad (The Coqui) The coquis whistled me asleep every night, a choir that came back home with me. Clacking keychains, the lapel button next to the Puerto Rican flag. Now, the frogs are fewer or did I remember them in grander numbers? Back home, I looked but could not find them hugged to the dark side of trees.

Autoridad (Nobody) Left blank until I return to get it stamped again. Blank until the coquis find the island song again. Open until my father and I take one last trip.

PLATANAL

After Myrna Báez

The folded leaves umbrella over
fruits slow and hard
to replenish with nothing
but the tamp of jibaro hands
and the care of their machetes.

The umbelled landscape layers
a sunless orange sky
above smoky hills that
should be green,
and analog bars that should be
on a TV set, hold the scene intact.
Where the jungle becomes
a grey curtain, hints of poles
stand without barb wire,
and beneath are the starch, protein,
and soft flesh to be savored
mostly by those who can only taste
from that place so far out of memory,
it's almost called to mind.

FISH HOOK

I was five when I learned my own blood.
Dad and I fished the lake of cement slabs,
out past yellow grass, our feet jammed in mud.
I pulled the snagged line. Snapped back. The hook stabbed
my thumb, slid past bone, dented the fingernail.
The sun's search for horizon came about
reflecting filament line, a detail
like dad dropping the bucket of caught trout.

Everything halted: the water still cold,
red salmon eggs stuck on our hooks for bait.
He steadied my hand—shaking, uncontrolled.
Father worked the hook. Barbs excavated
through skin ripped. For the tiny hole, I cried,
the blood pooled in our hands I could not guide.

GARTER SNAKES

We watched other creatures
scatter and insects
burrow from
light overbearing. The garter snakes
under lifted boards
in a field glide tall grass to escape.

"Grab the tail before it turns,"
the mantra that prevented
the clampdown of small jaws,
out-of-nowhere bites
on fingers
from tiny, pink mouths.

I never feared snakes but dreaded
friends who inflicted
commandments of childhood

that smashed heads,
that lacerated black and yellow lines
into sinews and split ligaments.
I hated the terrifying red, speckling
rocks and dirt, clashing
with our youth.
When I threw rocks, I missed

on purpose. In the arroyo with the shallow
creek and the broken bridge,
I watched freed snakes
ripple atop shallow water
with their heads level—
a holy incident
we did not yet know
we envied.

GRATITUDE

They never meant to save you
when they bludgeoned you
with the punches and kicks
that left them panting
as they ruffled your pockets,
slipped cash from your wallet,
and deserted you on the side street.

You disappear into the canned cylinder
to drown in the MRI's humming
that finds the terminal mass
in your brain. A skull fracture,
brain swelling, and broken ribs
should not be a miracle.

You hear the intern tell the technician,
"God works in mysterious ways,"
while your assailants drink
in an empty bar across town
with little remorse for giving
you another day. And you're left asking,
how do you thank
them for beating the cancer out of you
like a bloody hundred dollar bill
they'll never spend?

SYMPATHY FOR THE COCKROACH

The exterminator sprayed the house down
and sent the roaches scurrying into their slow
halt, away from the swirling mist of death,
and the whole time he described the different types,
telling me it's a good thing the flying ones
aren't here. I noticed one roach
sputtering toward a table's unreachable
safety, the exterminator soaked him and watched it
like a man drowning in cheap cologne.
When I asked if I should kill it, the cockroach with
antennaeshakingthinlegstwitchingonhisbackwrithing,
the exterminator told me to let it suffer.
Even though I can't stand roaches
I lingered until the exterminator
moved on before putting my shoe down on the roach
and snuffing it out of misery, wondering
if it would free me from my daily agonies
and do the same for me.

MY FATHER THROWING AWAY HIS FLIP FLOPS

He slips them off
to reveal
indented footprints
embedded dark on paper-thin soles,
smooth as apple's flesh.
Black straps stretched
but intact.

They collected
soil samples—
Vietnam, Panama,
Puerto Rico, Germany—
never catalogued
during years of military service from
countries I may never know.
I'm asking, what does it say
about a man
who can wear
flip-flops
for thirty-seven years

then say farewell
by clapping them together twice
and discarding them
with other things
destined for landfill?

ARS POETICA

When you pace your hallways and wish the walls would say something
back.

When you can't stop bad-mouthing your handwriting.

When ancestral light circles you and seizes your pen.

When you speak the native tongue you've never learned.

When it infuriates the phantoms to be engineered into prose instead of
poems.

When you smell of fire wrapped around you on a rainy day.

When you wish you had listened to your elders speak the old customs.

When you collect ghosts in a jar before they slip out the window.

When you approach shadows in your room's neglected corners,
shivering fright.

When you forgive the spirits who cannot find the courage to tap your
shoulder.

When you figure out the specters sporting toothy grins are inside you.

When you go back to tossing in bed to recite and forget lines.

SCARS

My body is the calendar of spills
that cannot be mopped away
like footprints tracked into my house.
My upper lip with two almost matching—
an origin story of stitches
for a wailing child
choking out the sobs of a furnace in
a wicked city.

I am not a quiet person, but I never
let anyone see
how the angry ones are stockpiled
with my smashed-open fists
against light switches and walls
I grudgingly repair,
how often I exhale
cuss words that gravitate me
toward cigarettes I'd like to snuff out on myself
to join the burns on my left forearm.

I come close but make myself latch onto
the ironic appreciation
scarred with the lovely photographs
of mistakes mapped along
my reckless body, exposed
like a rusted-out car in a dying lake.

FEAR OF HEIGHTS

It took my father two days
to down that tree with a machete.
Forty feet up, he hacked off limbs
and worked down.
Sap stuck to his gloves, seeping
on rungs and everything he touched

like the clouds of beetles
that consumed neighborhood trees.
When I felt the ladder's want to give,
I leaned my weight into gripping
with clenched knuckles. I studied his jammed feet
against the sides, reacting.
My father told me
any branch could be severed
with the proper slant.

Whenever he slashed,
my father wrapped one arm
around the ladder, the other chopping
through. Bark brushed
my face. I squinted. Larger branches
groaned with my father's

gradual steps down. I inched
closer to ladder and trunk.
Sections of tree slammed
into the ground and ended
the quiet between us. When he reached

for the farthest branches,
I caught my stomach dropping
and looked away
from the ladder's bow, leaves
whirling green,
descending around me.

STILL LIFE WITH VULTURES ON A FENCE

My approach does not
rouse them. They rest all around my uncle's
goat pen, wings stretched wide as dull black
decorations of flight. Their pink heads
face toward the valley,
past the blasted weathervane across the highway,
toward the nearby shoreline of
the island. Their stillness strikes me
to wonder their intention in pose—
maybe menacing, perhaps warming up
for resumed migration, or stretching to wake.
I assume they roost on the island and
outnumber the local birds in the sky,
never considering PR as a stop in their journey
north, beyond the view of the coast.
They interrupt silent travel with their wings flapping
into ascent, scouting
for the local carrion,
nearby and out of sight,
and then they tilt wings again
to rise further and further out
of my view below. One of my cousins
calls my fellow travelers ugly as sin
but I have to disagree.

THE RIGHT WAY TO DIE FOR A POEM

Osip Mandelstam in a gulag for a cockroach written on Stalin's lip,
Garcia-Lorca buried where he fell for siding with those
who have nothing, Roque Dalton gunned down
by ERP comrades, and the Spanish writer I read about
accidently electrocuted by a hair dryer in her tub.
Thinking of them, I want to know if this
is the way I really want to go:
scribbling words about a shirtless man
on top of a southbound train
on the back of a gas receipt
against my steering wheel with both hands
at 80 miles-per-hour, praying a deer
will not cross the interstate and
wary of the strong, inspired gusts.

SQUIRREL WARS

On a day when he captures a squirrel in
a trash can cage,
my father douses her with water.
He shakes her around to the beat of screams
and bangs. She shivers and screeches,
a forty-minute interrogation he can't
but wants to end. My mother pleads for him
to free the squirrel, keeping her distance from
the violent stand-off in his little garden.
She's never seen his battle scars this close.

My dad is pent up, pissed off that
rubber snakes and pinwheels don't work.
He's counting missing peaches, devoured
blossoms, nibbled spinach, pinched
tomato stems. He sends the squirrels
into retreat with the artillery of
sprinklers, buckets, and shoes, but
they are stubborn like him.

Every day after he frees the squirrel,
my father seems older and quieter.
He still calls squirrels
the enemy, fuckers, sons of bitches, but now
he opens the back door and hesitates—
maybe my mom's asking him to give them a head start or
maybe he's thinking that same state of war
that make their hearts hammer.

CIVILIAN

After a photograph by Philip Jones Griffiths, 1967

After the American medic carried you
from that smoldered village, he cleaned
abrasions, bandaged over your face
and eyes. He left a point
of hair sticking out the back. You didn't know
the medic should have
tagged you *V.C.*, and, instead,
dressed you in a baggy shirt
and tied an ID to your arm.
Lost in burn marks and flash of hot smoke,
all you could do was touch
your charred hand
to your face for
the pain of a private portrait.

FOR THE UNDERDOGS

Like anyone, I've spent the last few years smelling failure
wafting off the politicians and blotting
onto newspapers that smudge my fingers.
The poems won't come tonight. I'm thinking instead
of this hiss of anti-war, shock and awe, Saddam statue yanked
to crack the tiles below. I shake my head for battles
fought for no resolve, and I have to ask if the occupation
turning out insurgents is anything like a failed revolt
tamped down and suddenly labeled terrorism.
I close my eyes in prayer for the underdogs, who
line up on both sides, who
also lament the civilian sisters and brothers,
traumatized by quiet nights and wishing
for uneventful trips to the market. I write
so something like hope emerges even when fears
emanate as burning tires and car alarm screams,
desensitized in the broadcast of our daily quagmires.

THE MARTYRS OF JULY 26, 1953

After René Mederos' Silk Screen #19

In the foreground, the first rebel
mortised, face down without shoes.
His rifle almost blends in the ground
and waits. We stop counting
the distant rebels who die
piled in orange, purple, pink
body smears
lying in a black field,
face up, bocarriba.

Ready to fall off the poster's edges,
all of them unfold their arms,
stretch their bodies, the cry for revolution
floating out of Moncada
past the soldiers in green uniforms
to all of the island's voiceless rebels
misplaced in thick ink.

REVISING SCARS

I bait my father with questions about his history
like the tattoos of two birds inked on in 1952
that I already assigned the meaning of young love
and longing and the preservation of him as a man,
symbolism as powerful as the shrapnel lingering
inside his body and Agent Orange on his limbs,
deeper than the cluttered drawer where he keeps
his two Purple Hearts, and he challenges family myth
when he tells me he was too drunk to remember
how those damned tattoos got on him in the first place.

WHAT I SAID ONE TIME WHEN A WOMAN CALLED ME JOSE

"Not all Mexicans are named Jose
and not all Mexicans are Mexican, and,
in fact, there are other countries
where they also speak Spanish,
and I am actually a U.S. citizen born in this country
and English is my first language."
I stopped when she apologized for being
inconsiderate, said it was an honest mistake,
and my mean streak kicked in to convert
her guilt into a seething sun's glare when I told her,
"That's okay, my middle name is Jose."

TO MY PARENTS, AFTER SURVIVING THE DRIVE
ON HIGHWAY 123

When we drove to the edge of Highway 10, in the middle
of the island, where the road abruptly stopped, marked by no signs and
only the valley's flooding river, my mother's repeated prayer
and my dad's cussing strung together with *hostia* and *carajo*
rode along with us through the heavy rainfall
that scared wipers to life. I didn't want to backtrack three hours
and gambled this stray highway, cut on sharp turns
and flimsy guardrails, would guide us back to the hotel.
I tried to camouflage my own fear of failing my parents
on an island where everyone insisted me a gringo. I pointed out
the rain forest panorama to our right and the orange and red flowers
as vibrant as opals in the storm. They pointed out less and fewer cars
going the same way. I muttered my own prayer for patience
under my breath in hopes they didn't notice my white knuckles
choking the rental car's steering wheel. The rain played a steady
torrent and the switchbacks stirred equally scary
mountain roads from Colorado inside memory.
I wanted to tell my parents to save prayers for another time
and stop mentioning the car accident we passed a few kilometers back.
I couldn't promise them much more than the rain
eventually ceasing, me driving us until we found our way to Ponce
or to another highway with numbers we could recognize,
the same way they could not promise to see me
as a son who could take care of them in this place so far from home.

IN MY HANDS

The mantis sways
with no influential
breeze. It is the delicate
texture of tree bark but a green body
with a dark circle on
its back. Praying arms pivot,
feelers opening.
The wings threaten to unfold.
It grazes my skin then
plants itself. The antennae twitch,
communicating
with a far off universe.
I stare past its mandibles and
into compound eyes, shade
of creamy jade, holding
an otherworldly specimen
in my hands.

NEW WORLD MAP

These are places marked by no plaque.
No committee petitions for historical status,
but something happened here—

a speech, a revolt, two people
embracing one last time,
unseen on any atlas. I'm surrounded
by land delicious with yellow grass
where others see thirst. I follow
dotted lines that scar paper and pass
peaks and waterways
to unidentified sites.

Landmarks formed as skin stretched over
bone and muscle in the chaos of anatomy,
lost under tracked-up dust.

If only I were a magician
with a metal detector personality,
who could conjure the coins of history
to surface. I don't want
to intrude on lecture hall frays
that debate the map's origins.
I want to stop scraping by
and satisfy this craving

a life of wandering maps
and whispered beginnings of epics
I will always struggle to write.

MY FATHER HAS A MENUDO STORY TOO

For Dan Vera

In Dan's version, his father is a Cuban in Texas,
and in mine, my father is a Puerto Rican in New York.
The island slang is the same, both men calling
loose change menudo, and both fathers slapping money
on the diner counter, asking, "Dame menudo, por favor."

Then, the story veers, yours is $5 and my father's is $10,
but it's still a lot of tripe, hominy, and spices stewed together.
Your father asked to carry it with his hands and then had friends
explain the mix-up. My father has no friends in
his version and ends up with a large bowl and the
cook promising more when he finishes. My father answers
with, "What the hell is that?" The story's punch line lands.

When you tell it, Dan, you mention exegesis,
the critical interpretation of the text, and I can see how we
share a coincidental story of our fathers, two islanders, far away
from home. We are two sons with our stories
flowing through us thicker than any sacred soup, warmer than
a son's memory of a father's hand resting on his shoulder.

OF FATHERS AND VOLCANOES

Mount St. Helens originally made dad
afraid to be the first Puerto Rican
killed in burning lava and blackened land.
He gave me ashes in three coffee cans
dusted off the cars and scooped up handfuls
on base, Ft. Lewis, in 1980,
and called it our history. In the pull
toward danger zones, seared away safety,
pops of skeletal steam will always feed
his volcanic anxiety denser
than the hot shadows of PTSD.
Until now, I was too young to be there,
to feel ash black sky and comb through the blast,
to help him pick up the glowing hurt last.

PUERTO RICAN CAREER PATH

Lajas, Puerto Rico, 1951-Colorado Springs, CO, 2005

My father's father told him, "If you're not in school,
I'll put you to work, pendejo."

At seventeen, my father hacked sugarcane and wore himself out all night
shooting pool and dice and fighting whoever he sharked for two years

until he walked off the island and into a green uniform. He wore it
in Korea, Vietnam, and for three decades a soldier.

For twenty years afterward, my father whistled to empty carts and
loaded washers in the hospital laundromat on the night shift.

Finally, at 73 years old, he didn't have to sweat fluorescent lights
or steam press scrubs or whorl the sheets in heavy water

or punch another goddamn timecard. "Son," he told me over a cup of
coffee, "I don't want to be a rich American. I'm a rich Puerto Rican."

AN APOLOGY TO LA ISLA

I implicate myself for neglecting
the island, Puerto Rico, home of my
father, half of my blood, land voiced in dropped
syllable's Andalusian Spanish, isla
I haven't seen in too many years.

I hear hesitation of each coqui's
whistle sent to quell the night, the racket
of bugs bumped against the mosquito nets,
tiny lizards stitched along the house walls.
I've spent too much time away and clung to

my landlocked home state and obsessed over
how las montañas in my mom's Ecuador
dominates the view. I need to smell
empanadilla shacks feeding outlying
towns, try to sleep the humidity's torment,

drown in the hibiscus that color the
lush forests, coax out the island inside.
I will sacrifice a plantain in your
honor and fail to cook a passable
batch of arroz con gandules and wash it down in

liters of cola champagne and accept
that I am a tourist who will ask for
forgiveness only after I return
to PR and say it en español
without tripping on any syllables.

This Valdivian stone figure dates back to around 3,500-2,000 B.C. on the Santa Elena peninsula near the modern-day town of Valdivia, Ecuador.

Photo courtesy of Patti Freeman Schreiber.

Juan Morales is the author the chapbook, *The Ransom and Example of Atahualpa*, and the collection, *Friday and the Year That Followed*, winner of the 2005 Rhea Seymour and Gorsline Poetry Prize. His poetry has appeared in *Acentos Review, Copper Nickel, Crab Orchard Review, Huizache, North Dakota Review, Palabra, Poet Lore, Sugar House Review, Washington Square, Zone 3*, and others. He is the Editor/Publisher of *Pilgrimage Magazine*, a CantoMundo Fellow, and an Associate Professor of English at Colorado State University-Pueblo, where he directs the Creative Writing Program and curates the SoCo Reading Series.

PRAISE FOR THE SIREN WORLD

Juan J. Morales writes: "It takes a thousand voices to tell a single story," which is another way of saying, "It took a thousand journeys to get to mine." As an artist with Ecuadorian and Puerto Rican bloodlines engaged with the Spanish colonial histories of South America and the Caribbean, Morales explores the legacies of language and landscape, mapping out an expansive poetic portrait of his ancestral homeland. *The Siren World* is a glorious testimony to the will of the Americas to reconfigure and preserve its cultural identities, which are still thriving and palpable in the heartbeats and "reconstruction songs" of its native children, its travelers, its bordercrossers, and its poets.

—Rigoberto González

In *The Siren World*, Juan J. Morales explores the complexities of identity with grace and humor, passion and irony, arcing across centuries through lessons never learned, voices never heard. Caught between multiple worlds, multiple identities both mistaken and claimed, he offers a unique perspective that challenges many of our assumptions as readers. He may be someone "who speaks the native tongue" he's "never learned," but he is fluent in the language of poetry. History does indeed come alive in these poems that remind us that we are still living it, and reliving it, moving back, forward, then back again, no matter who we are—and, as Morales reminds us, we're all still trying to figure that out too.

—Jim Daniels

The word "cleave" has two seemingly paradoxical meanings: to divide, and to join. In *The Siren World*, Juan Morales defines a series of distances--from Ecuador to Puerto Rico, from mother to father, from the historical pain of a smallpox victim to the "failed double-kick flip, ankle's loud pop" of a skateboarding accident. On one page, Pizarro and his generals sort the "wreckage of job well done," and on the next we confront "The Cursing Chorus of the Mob." But these poems are about bridges, not canyons; they do not gape, they reach. They sing, and they code switch, as in "Passport": "When I turned 18, my father gave me a machete. When I turned 21, my father gave me a shoe shine kit." Morales showcases his striking dexterity of craft, toggling between prose poetry and sonnets, and a genuine search for truth no matter how painful. Yet there is pleasure here too, in the euphoria of the moment "When ancestral light circles you and seizes your pen." I am grateful for this voice, and for this brave and bracing collection.

—Sandra Beasley